I0435259

TURKEY

Sandie Lee Books

Thanks for checking out the Sandie Lee Books Series. Please note: All Rights Reserved. No part of this publication may be reproduced in any form or by any means, including scanning, photocopying, or otherwise without prior written permission of the copyright holder. Copyright © 2014

Turkey

The turkey belongs to the Meleagris genus. Even though there are many different breeds of the turkey, there are only two species; domesticated and wild. The word "turkey" is derived from the word "tuka." This means peacock in India. Some domesticated turkeys are raised for food and others for pets. These are cousins to the wild turkey. Let's explore more fun facts about this bird. We will discover where it lives in the wild, some of its behaviors and other fascinating facts. So read on...

Where in the World?

Did you know the domesticated turkey can be found in many parts of the world? These turkeys live on farms where they are bred for the meat industry. Wild turkeys are mainly found in North America. These turkeys spend their time in the forests of this region where they are safer from predators.

The Body of a Turkey

Did you know the wild turkey is smaller than a tame one? The wild male turkey can weigh from 8 to 24 pounds. Tame turkeys can reach sizes of up to 86 pounds. The turkey is covered with feathers except for its head, neck, legs and feet. The male turkey has a waddle - extra flap of skin under its chin.

What a Turkey Eats

Did you know the wild turkey is an omnivore? This means it will eat both protein and veggies. The turkey will eat nuts like acorns, hickory and beech nuts. Plus, grains like corn and wheat and fruit such as berries, wild grapes and crabapples. For protein it will hunt small reptiles and snakes, insects, worms and slugs.

The Turkey's Special Ability

Did you know the turkey can blush? When a turkey is upset, angry, sick, scared or excited the skin on its neck and head will change color. It can turn from a pale pink or bluish-grey color to red, blue or white. In the mating season, the male's waddle will turn a bright red color.

The Turkey as Prey

Did you know the wild turkey has plenty of pred-ators? The eggs of a wild turkey are the most likely to get eaten. Animals such as snakes, raccoons, skunks, crows and coyotes will all hunt for wild turkey eggs. Young turkeys may be preyed upon by eagles, hawks, owls, cougars and foxes.

Turkey Talk

Did you know the female turkey only clucks and cackles? The real talkers among the turkey group is the male. In fact, he is called, a gobbler, because of the sound he makes. A male will use a loud, shrill throaty call that lasts about a second. He can also cackle and purr when on the ground.

The Turkey's Stomach

Did you know the turkey has 2 stomachs? The turkey has an extra stomach called, the gizzard. Part of the turkey's diet is to eat small stones. These smooth pebbles fall into the gizzard. Since the turkey has no teeth, the gizzard acts as a way of further breaking down the turkey's food.

Turkey Mom

Did you know the female turkey is called a hen? The breeding season of the wild turkey is from March to April. The female turkey is attracted to a male by his show of feathers and the way he struts. After the hen has built a nest, she will lay from 8 to 16 eggs in one sitting.

Baby Turkey

Did you know a baby turkey is called, a poult? Wild baby turkeys are hatched covered with fuzzy feathers. They can vary in color, but usually have stripes on them. They are able to walk and feed themselves the day after they hatch. At night, the hen will sit on her poults to keep them safe and warm.

The Turkey at Rest

Did you know the wild turkey can fly? A wild turkey can fly in short bursts. In fact, when evening comes, it will fly high up into a tree for the night. This is called, roosting. The wild turkey will sleep in a flock. Before coming down from the tree in the morning, the turkey will make a soft call to the rest of the group.

Life of a Turkey

Did you know a wild turkey can live to be over 12 years-old? Due to the many predators the turkey has, most of them do not make it out of the egg stage. However, if left alone, a healthy turkey can live to a ripe old-age. However, most of this species will only live to be about 3 years-old.

Royal Palm Turkey

This turkey is tame and is usually kept as a pet. It has beautiful white feathers with bands of metallic black on its chest and rump area. This bird can grow to be around 22 pounds for males and 12 pounds for females. The male of this breed is very docile and the hens make great moms.

Eastern Wild Turkey

This wild turkey is the most common. It can be found in the eastern half of the United States. The eastern wild turkey is one of the largest subspecies. Males can grow to be around 2.5 feet tall and weigh more than 20 pounds. Its feathers are a rich mixture of brown, black, white and metallic copper colors.

Gould's Wild Turkey

The gould's turkey may be the least known. It can be found in Arizona and New Mexico. This turkey breed has longer legs and bigger feet than most other turkeys. Its tail feathers are also larger than most. Its body can be blue-green in color, with bright white tips on its tail feathers.

Quiz

Question 1: How big can some tame turkeys get?

Answer 1: Around 86 pounds

Question 2: Where do turkeys get their protein from?

Answer 2: Small reptiles, snakes, insects, worms and slugs.

Question 3: Where is the male turkey's *waddle* located?

Answer 3: On its neck

Question 4: What is a male turkey called that is also like the sound he makes?

Answer 4: *A gobbler*

Question 5: What is special about the turkey's stomach?

Answer 5: It has two of them

Thank you for checking out another addition from Sandie Lee Books! Make sure to check out Amazon.com for many other great titles.

www.ingramcontent.com/pod-product-compliance
Lightning Source LLC
Chambersburg PA
CBHW050802290526
45792CB00008B/2300